Given to me by Michiko in
June of 1982

You Are Always My Friend

It is comforting
to know that we are friends;
that we can share our thoughts
    with each other in confidence,
that we can listen and care
    for each other with love
        and concern.
It makes my heart glad
    to know that we are friends.
And I want to tell you
    how much I care and
    how often I am thinking of you.

—Doris Amundson Arnold

Other books by

Blue Mountain Press INC

Come Into the Mountains, Dear Friend
by Susan Polis Schutz
I Want to Laugh, I Want to Cry
by Susan Polis Schutz
Peace Flows from the Sky
by Susan Polis Schutz
Someone Else to Love
by Susan Polis Schutz
I'm Not That Kind of Girl
by Susan Polis Schutz
Yours If You Ask
by Susan Polis Schutz
Love, Live and Share
by Susan Polis Schutz
The Language of Friendship
The Language of Love
The Language of Happiness
The Desiderata of Happiness
by Max Ehrmann
I Care About Your Happiness
by Kahlil Gibran/Mary Haskell
I Wish You Good Spaces
Gordon Lightfoot
We Are All Children Searching for Love
by Leonard Nimoy
Come Be with Me
by Leonard Nimoy
Creeds to Love and Live By
On the Wings of Friendship
You've Got a Friend
Carole King
With You There and Me Here
The Dawn of Friendship
Once Only
by jonivan
Expressing Our Love
You and Me Against the World
Paul Williams
Words of Wisdom, Words of Praise
Reach Out for Your Dreams
I Promise You My Love
Thank You for Being My Parents
A Mother's Love
A Friend Forever
gentle freedom, gentle courage
diane westlake
When We Are Apart
It's Nice to Know Someone Like You
by Peter McWilliams

You Are
Always
My Friend

A collection of poems on friendship
Edited by Susan Polis Schutz

Blue Mountain Press ™

Boulder, Colorado

Library of Congress Number: 81-68584
ISBN: 0-88396-150-4

Manufactured in the United States of America
First Printing: September, 1981

The following works have previously appeared in Blue Mountain Arts publications:

"You know how I feel," by Susan Polis Schutz. Copyright © Continental Publications, 1972. "Someone," by Susan Polis Schutz. Copyright © Continental Publications, 1973. "Though we drifted," "There is no need," and "Sometimes," by Susan Polis Schutz. Copyright © Continental Publications, 1974. "You are a free person," by Susan Polis Schutz. Copyright © Continental Publications, 1975. "It is a rare and special thing," by Ruth Langdon Morgan; "A Friend Like You," by Henry V. Rutherford; "When we lived," by Susan Polis Schutz; and "The memories that friends," by Rebecca J. Barrett. Copyright © Continental Publications, 1979. "Friendship is a special blessing," by Iverson Williams. Copyright © Iverson Williams, 1979. "A friend is," by Susan Polis Schutz. Copyright © Stephen Schutz and Susan Polis Schutz, 1980. "As a friend," and "Our Friendship," by Laine Parsons. Copyright © Blue Mountain Arts, Inc., 1980. "I know it might sound a little funny," "A friendship as cherished," and "To have a friend like you," by Andrew Tawney; "Sometimes," "Being friends," "You mean so much to me," and "There are so many people," by Jamie Delere; "Your friendship. . ." by Laine Parsons; and "The person who wrote," and "If it weren't for," by Michael Rille. Copyright © Blue Mountain Arts, Inc., 1981. All rights reserved. Reprinted by permission.

Thanks to the Blue Mountain Arts creative staff.

Acknowledgments appear on page 92

Blue Mountain Press INC

P.O. Box 4549, Boulder, Colorado 80306

CONTENTS

A friend is
someone who is concerned
with everything you do

A friend is
someone to call upon
during good and bad times

A friend is
someone who understands
whatever you do

A friend is
someone who tells you
the truth about yourself . . .

A friend is
someone who knows
what you are going through
at all times

A friend is
someone who does not
compete with you

A friend is
someone who is genuinely happy
for you when things go well

A friend is
someone who tries to
cheer you up when
things don't go well

A friend is
an extension of yourself
without which
you are not complete

Thank you for being my friend

—Susan Polis Schutz

Everyone needs at least
  one good, close friend;
one who means a lot,
and who can share secrets
and feelings
that might otherwise be
locked up and afraid to come out.
Everyone needs someone
who cares—and doesn't hide it;
someone to ease the down moods.
Thank you . . . for being the one for me.
I hope my friendship has been
at least half as good for you,
because friends as special as you
are hard to find.

—Barbara Gladys

$\mathbf{S}$omehow,
a simple "thank you"
doesn't really measure up
to what I'd like to say and give
   for everything you've given me.
I think, maybe,
   that a rainbow
   or a jar of moonbeams
   would be more appropriate.
I only wish
   I had them to give to you.
Until then, I thank you
from the bottom of my heart.

—Debbie Avery

I ask myself
why I have been
   blessed with someone
   so understanding
   and so caring . . .
Perhaps it's because
I can truly appreciate you
or maybe it's because
   God knew
   I needed you
   so much.

                    —Jean Therese

I know it might sound a little funny
   at first,
but it's really true,
and I want you to know—
that having you in my life
   is really enough for me
      to be happy . . .

Sometimes it seems like
everyone talks of "needing this"
      and "wanting that . . ."
And seems to fill their days
   with thoughts of acquiring new things
   for themselves, and of attaching a lesser
   value to the things they already have
   that are really so valuable
      and so important .

But when I think about it,
when I think of what really matters to me,
my thoughts always return
   to the one most important aspect
      of my life—
without which all the other things
   I have and hold would be meaningless.

I have been blessed with much . . .
and even though I may not always be
as content as I should be,
underneath it all
I realize how very gracious
   life has been for me,
and how very wonderful
   tomorrow hopes to be.

For I have you in my life . . .
   and that's enough for me.

—Andrew Tawney

My friend,
we have come such a long way
in the time that we've
   known each other.
We've given each other encouragement
and have accomplished things
that we never thought we could do.
I have become a better person
   since knowing you.
You have given me many things
which I will treasure for a lifetime,
and the most important thing of all
   is the gift of your friendship.

—Laura Lee Leyman

What is a Friend

What is a friend? I will tell you. It is a person with whom you dare to be yourself. Your soul can be naked with him. He seems to ask of you to put on nothing, only to be what you are. He does not want you to be better or worse. When you are with him, you feel as a prisoner feels who has been declared innocent. You do not have to be on your guard. You can say what you think, so long as it is genuinely you. He understands those contradictions in your nature that lead others to misjudge you. With him you breathe freely. You can avow your little vanities and envies and hates and vicious sparks, your meannesses and absurdities and, in opening them up to him, they are lost, dissolved on the white ocean of his loyalty. He understands. You do not have to be careful. You can abuse him, neglect him, tolerate him. Best of all, you can keep still with him. It makes no matter. He likes you—he is like fire that purges to the bone. He understands. He understands. You can weep with him, sing with him, laugh with him, pray with him. Through it all—and underneath—he sees, knows and loves you. A friend? What is a friend? Just one, I repeat, with whom you dare to be yourself.

—C. Raymond Beran

Friendship defies age
and ignores distance.
It weathers the hard times
and shares the good.
Together we have found this.
Our friendship has provided acceptance
and understanding in a world
that pushes people apart.
But I will always remain
with the memories
of the times we have shared
knowing how fortunate I am
to be able to call you my friend.

—Cindy Yrun

A Friend Like You

A friend is someone with whom
you can be completely honest
and who understands you
just the way you are.

A friend is someone to talk to
when things are going wrong
and who will give you support
in times of need.

It's wonderful to have
a friend like you.

—Henry V. Rutherford

I think of you
as a very special, dear friend . . .
in a place I hold in my heart
    for just a very few.
You came into my life
    offering happiness
    with caring underneath.
And I find myself responding
    in the same manner.
It is so easy to talk with you
    about things that sometimes are hard,
    and about things that sometimes I
    I have kept well hidden . . .
        even from myself . . .

You seem to be able to draw that out of me,
    and I think that maybe
        I am able to do that for you.
What a beautiful way
    to have
        and build
            a friendship.

—Sue Mitchell

I thank you . . .
for all the goodness,
kindness, honesty
and warmth of feeling
that the continuance
of our friendship brings.

—Franz Liszt

Every friendship
that lasts is
built of certain
durable materials.
The first of these
is truthfulness.
If I can look
into the eyes
of my friend and
speak out always
the truthful thought
and feeling
with the simplicity
of a little child,
there will be
a real friendship
between us.

—Bertha Conde

Sometimes
when I have something to tell you,
I hesitate—and wonder . . .
just how much of my feelings
I should allow to be seen,
and how you'll react to my words.

I know that I shouldn't be afraid
to tell you anything . . .
but I'm still sort of new
at being in this situation,
and I feel a little uneasy about
saying just whatever's on my mind.
But you know, don't you . . .
   of my feelings for you,
      whether they're spoken or not . . .
and my desire to open up to you
   with trust
      and with love.

—Jamie Delere

It is a rare and special thing
to find a friend who will remain
a friend forever.

—Ruth Langdon Morgan

Our Friendship

Every day of our friendship is as
exciting as the first rays of a new dawn.
Time may pass and space may
separate us, but distance cannot
alter feelings and trust between
true friends who realize that the same
sun shines on us all and the same
common bond is felt in the heart.
As our friendship grows and days
become years, we will look at our
friendship as a priceless gift given
to our yesterdays and waiting for
our tomorrows.

—Laine Parsons

. . .remember me,
as I do you,
with all the tenderness
which it is possible for one
to feel for another,
which no time can obliterate,
no distance alter,
but which is always the same.

—Abigail Adams

You
are
a
free
person.
I am so happy
because in your
freedom, you
choose me to
be your friend.

—Susan Polis Schutz

Being friends
comes so naturally to us—
We're always there for each other,
and it's never a chore, it's done
        from desire;
never an effort, but always a pleasure.
We've been friends
for quite awhile now,
and I'm sure that you know what I mean
when I say that
    the memories that we've got
are some of the finest I ever
        hope to have.

It makes me glad to think
that you'll be with me
    and I'll be with you
        as friends . . .

to face the new times ahead,
  to share the wonders they will bring,
    to confront whatever trials they may hold.

It's nice to know
  you'll always have me
  caring for you,
and I'll always have you
  just a thought away.

—Jamie Delere

The person who wrote
"Friend—is the most beautiful
   word in our language"
must have had a wonderful friend . . .
someone just as special
   as you are to me.

—Michael Rille

Friendship is a special blessing
from above. It's the sharing of
activities with someone who
understands and cares. It's a warm
ray of sunshine that fills our hearts
in times of need. It's the bringing
out of beautiful things in each
other that no one else looked hard
enough to find. It's
the mutual trust
and honesty that
lets us be
ourselves
at all times.

—Iverson Williams

Being a friend
comes naturally.
It is taking a moment
   out of your life
to give of yourself
by bringing comfort,
   encouragement and peace.

You do it graciously . . .
and I thank you.

—Linda DuPuy Moore

So often I sit and think
about the way things were —
The fun and friends,
the joy we all had
    and the times of just being together . . .
Of course there were some days,
times we wondered how we made it.
But our friendship helped us through.

Now we may be separated,
but the bond is still there.
Friendship holds us
    together.

—Joyce Brink

Though we
   drifted apart in distance
I always
   think of you as being right here
Though we have different interests
our experiences are still the same
and though we
   have many new friends
it is our old and
   continuous friendship
that means the most to me

—Susan Polis Schutz

You mean so much to me —
   and I just wanted you to know
   how very much I care . . .

You mean so much to me —
   you've helped me to find
   a special outlook on life
   that was hiding
   deep inside of me,
   waiting just for someone like you
   to open the door
   and set it free

You mean so much to me —
   for you've been there,
   through the good times and the bad,
   drying the tears and
   holding back the loneliness —
   giving me a friendly shoulder
   to lean on
   and enough smiles to last a lifetime . . .

You mean so much to me —
　　and I can't help but feel
　　as though I owe you so much more
　　than I can ever repay
　　But if there's a way —
　　any way
　　to hold and to help,
　　to provide and to encourage,
　　to give even a part of what
　　you have blessed me with,
　　I will be there for you

And wherever time will take us . . .
　　wherever we may be,
　　I always want you
　　　to remember
　　how much
　　you mean to me.

—Jamie Delere

i pray
that i am as much for you
as you are for me
my friend i love you

—diane westlake

As a friend
　　I've loved you lonely
　　and wanted you happy
　　I've thought of you often
　　and wanted to hold you
　　so many times
But as a dreamer
　　I simply hoped that you
　　would sense my caring
　　and imagined that you
　　would understand me
　　and thought that maybe
You know how much I care
　　though I've never taken
　　the time to tell you
　　how much you are cherished

—Laine Parsons

A friendship as cherished as ours
is more than just a closeness of two people . . .
it's an endearing bond felt and given,
and one of the most
important aspects of our lives.

A friendship
as secure as ours
is more than just a feeling . . .
it's a knowing and a being,
a knowledge that each will
always be there for the other
for as long as time will allow
and as strong as our hearts will permit . . .

A friendship
as rewarding as ours
is more than just an experience . . .
it's an event that is shared
by two fortunate people,
given the opportunity to
travel together through this
journey of life.

A friendship
as abundant as ours
is the most beautiful present
you could offer me,
and the greatest gift
I could ever receive.

—Andrew Tawney

You . . .
know how I feel
about you,
and always shall.

No one
 can ever
take your
 place
with me.

—Edna St. Vincent Millay

Being a friend . . .
is not having to worry where to begin,
feeling the warmth and trust within
A smile grown on one face
and mirrored on the other,
sharing personal thoughts
and listening . . . really listening
Chasing the shadows that get in the way,
being content and in love
   with the day
in the life of a friend
as wonderful
as you.

—Dorie Runyon

Because of a Friend

Life is a sweeter, stronger, fuller,
more gracious thing
for the friend's existence,
whether he be near or far.
If the friend is close at hand,
that is best; but if he is far away
he is still there to think of,
to wonder about, to hear from, to write to,
to share life and experience with,
to serve, to honor, to admire, to love.

—Arthur Christopher Benson

There are so many people
   in the world—
but there is only a handful,
a few precious individuals
that will ever become our friends,
and fewer still
that will remain our friends
   through life.
And of all the people in the world,
   you and I
have become friends
   in a wonderful way,
for a lifetime, together . . .
for a lifetime to stay.

—Jamie Delere

When we lived
near each other
we participated in
the same activities
Our friendship was
strong
because we shared
so many things
Now—living apart
we rarely
see each other
but our friendship is
even stronger
because we share
the same feelings
This closeness
of hearts
is what makes
a lifetime friendship
like ours

—Susan Polis Schutz

The memories that friends
have made together
grow stronger
with every passing day.

—Rebecca J. Barrett

What greater thing
is there
for two human souls
than to feel that they
are joined for life—
to strengthen each other
in all labor,
to rest on each other
in all sorrow,
to minister
to each other
in all pain,
and to be
with each other
in silent
unspeakable memories . . .

—George Eliot

It takes more than words
to let you know
how much it means to me
to have you as a friend
I can depend on you for understanding
when I am confused
I can depend on you for comfort
when I am sad
I can depend on you for laughter
when I am happy
I am so thankful
to know that you are
always
my friend

—Susan Polis Schutz

Friends,
no matter how
far separated,
will grow
in love
and sympathy
and nearness
to each other.

—Bertha Conde

You know that however much time
passes without your hearing
from me, there is not a day
that does not in some way or other
bring me nearer to you
or remind me
of your friendship.

—F. Mendelssohn

Thank you for your
presence in my life . . .
you encourage me to go
beyond myself.

—Linda DuPuy Moore

You're that special kind of friend
that everyone wishes they could have.
I always know when we're apart
     that we're still so close,
and when we're together
our time will be spent
     enjoying it to the fullest.

It's not everyone that can
     have a special friend
          like you.
I'm proud to say
     that I do.

—Teresa M. Fox

What a great blessing is a friend . . .
with a heart so trusty,
you may safely bury your secrets;
whose conscience you may
     fear less than your own;
who can relieve your cares
          by his conversation,
your doubts by his counsels,
your sadness by his good humor;
and whose very looks
give you comfort.
What a great blessing
          is a friend.

—Seneca

Your friendship . . .
holds a special place in my heart

—Laine Parsons

A friend is one
to whom one may pour
out all the contents
of one's heart,
chaff and grain together
knowing that the
gentlest of hands
will take and sift it,
keep what is worth keeping
and with a breath of kindness
blow the rest away.

—Arabian Proverb

You are always
so understanding
You are always
so concerned
You are always
so caring
You are always
so giving
You are always
so helpful
But most important
you are always
my
friend

—Susan Polis Schutz

Friends
are the leaves
of the tree
of life.

—George Meredith

Never shall I forget
the days which I spent
with you . . .
Continue to be my friend,
as you will always
find me yours.

—Ludwig van Beethoven

The most
I can do for
my friend is
simply to be
his friend.

—Henry David Thoreau

There is no need for
an outpouring of words
to explain oneself
to a friend.
Friends understand each
other's thoughts even
before they are spoken.

—Susan Polis Schutz

I simply want you
to know how nice
things have been
since I met you,
how very special it is
to spend time with you,
and how much better
life seems
with you in my world.

—Rowland R. Hoskins, Jr.

Friends are . . .
the kisses at hellos and goodbyes,
the feeling of never having been apart
because it's so great to be together,
the knowing that you
will find each other
no matter what happens
in this world, because no barrier
is strong enough
to dare separate you.

Friends are forever.

—Edith Schaffer Lederberg

You know how I feel
You listen to how I think
You understand . . .

You're
my
friend

—Susan Polis Schutz

Someone—
to talk with
to dance with
to sing with
to eat with
to laugh with
to cry with
to think with
to understand
Someone—
to be my friend

—Susan Polis Schutz

for the freedom
   to be as I am . . .
for the inspiration to be more . . .
for the confidence
   that I can do much,
for the renewed desire
   to reach my potential . . .
for the willingness
   to acknowledge my needs . . .
for the greater awareness
   of the needs and
      potentials of others . . .
for all that you have meant to me . . .
   I am grateful.

—Ellen Erlanger

If I could give you all there was
   in the world to give,
   it would never be enough,
   not for you . . .
You deserve all there is, and more.
I can only hope
   that in some small way
      you know
I give you my best.

—Noreen Jenney

My Friend . . .

I offer you laughter
   for laughter is beauty.
I offer you honesty
   for honesty is pure.
I offer you patience
   for patience is needed to gain trust.
I offer sincerity
   for through my sincerity I will show
   you my inner being and desires . . .
All I ask in return
   is for you to be honest and open
      for through your honesty and
      openness
I will receive from you
   all that I offer.

—Roger C. Van Horn

If it weren't for
special friends like you . . .

the world would have
   no rainbows.
Thanks for lighting up my life.

—Michael Rille

... You know that nothing can ever change what we have always been and always will be to each other.

—Franklin D. Roosevelt

FRIEND

Friend, we've laughed
  When humor had
  Passed
Friend, you listened with
  Closed lips while
  Opening your heart
Friend, you felt my sorrow
  And we formed one
  Tear
Friend, these things
  I'll remember as
  The thought of you
  Warms my heart.

—Lanny Allen

To have a friend like you
to cherish and keep
beyond the miles,
To have someone to keep in touch with
as the days turn into years,
To have a companion so close and trusting
that you can speak of your troubles
and share your greatest hopes,
To have a person who means so much
that you would just like to
thank them for being
in your thoughts,
Is to have a special blessing
for a richer existence
and the knowledge that happiness
will never leave your side

—Andrew Tawney

Friends are not only together
when they are side-by-side,
even one who is far away . . .
is still in our thoughts.

—Ludwig van Beethoven

Sometimes
when I am
sitting alone
I think of you

Sometimes
when I am
out with a lot
of people
I think of you

Always when I
want to talk
to someone
I think of you

—Susan Polis Schutz

Don't walk in front of me
   I may not follow
Don't walk behind me
   I may not lead
Walk beside me
And just be my friend

—Albert Camus

Friend . . .

Who you are and what you mean to me
are expressions of what
 life means to me.
I am thankful that in this time
 our paths merge.
Only the future knows
how long we will travel the same ways,
certain only that our lives will be changed
because of our common experiences.

Let's enjoy the walk together
 and celebrate
the person each of us brings to the journey
and the friends we are becoming
along the way.

—Nancy Ferrell

I love you,
Not only for what you are
But for what I am
When I am with you.

I love you
Not only for what
You have made of yourself
But for what
You are making of me.

I love you
For the part of me
That you bring out;
I love you
For putting your hand
Into my heaped-up heart
And passing over
All the foolish, weak things
That you can't help
Dimly seeing there,
And for drawing out
Into the light
All the beautiful belongings
That no one else had looked
Quite far enough to find.

I love you because you
Are helping me to make
Of the lumber of my life
Not a tavern
But a temple;
Out of works
Of my every day
Not a reproach
But a song.

I love you
Because you have done
More than any creed
Could have done
To make me good,
And more than any fate
Could have done
To make me happy.

You have done it
Without a touch,
Without a word,
Without a sign.
You have done it
By being yourself.
Perhaps that is what
Being a friend means,
After all.

—Roy Croft

ACKNOWLEDGMENTS

We gratefully acknowledge the permission granted by the following authors, publishers and authors' representatives to reprint poems and excerpts from their publications.

Doris Amundson Arnold for "It is comforting." Copyright © Doris Amundson Arnold, 1981. All rights reserved. Reprinted by permission.

Debbie Avery for "Somehow." Copyright © Debbie Avery, 1981. All rights reserved. Reprinted by permission.

Laura Lee Leyman for "My friend." Copyright © Laura Lee Leyman, 1981. All rights reserved. Reprinted by permission.

Jean Therese for "I ask myself." Copyright © Jean Therese, 1981. All rights reserved. Reprinted by permission.

Cindy Yrun for "Friendship defies age." Copyright © Cindy Yrun, 1980. All rights reserved. Reprinted by permission.

Barbara Gladys for "Everyone needs at least." Copyright © Barbara Gladys, 1981. All rights reserved. Reprinted by permission.

Sue Mitchell for "I think of you." Copyright © Sue Mitchell, 1981. All rights reserved. Reprinted by permission.

Linda DuPuy Moore for "Being a friend" and "Thank you for your presence." Copyright © Linda DuPuy Moore, 1980. All rights reserved. Reprinted by permission.

Joyce Brink for "So often I sit and think." Copyright © Joyce Brink, 1981. All rights reserved. Reprinted by permission.

Diane Westlake for "i pray." Copyright © Diane Westlake, 1977. All rights reserved. Reprinted by permission.

John Schaffner for "You know how I feel," by Edna St. Vincent Millay. From the book LETTERS OF EDNA ST. VINCENT MILLAY, edited by Allan Ross Macdougall. Published by Harper & Brothers. © Copyright 1952 by Norma Millay Ellis. © Copyright 1952 by Allan Ross Macdougall. All rights reserved. Reprinted by permission.